Heady Scent of Lilac

A Collection of Romantic Poetry and Art

Dorothy Atkins

Heady Scent of Lilac

Copyright © 2019 by Dorothy Atkins
All rights reserved

ISBN: 978-0-578-21630-0
Library of Congress: TX 8-716-123

Published by Dorothy Atkins, San Jose, California, 95132.

Printed in the United States of America.

PUBLISHER'S NOTE: All rights reserved. No Part of this book may be reproduced in any form without permission in writing from the publisher.

Dorothy Atkins, Poetry and Art, San Jose, California 95132
Pat Auston, Line Drawings, Highlands Ranch, Colorado 80126
Luanna K. Leisure, Photographer, Campbell, California 95008

To order additional books go to: **http://www.LuLu.com**
or **Amazon.com.**

Email: **chabot50@sbcglobal.net**
http://www.dorothyatkinsartist.com

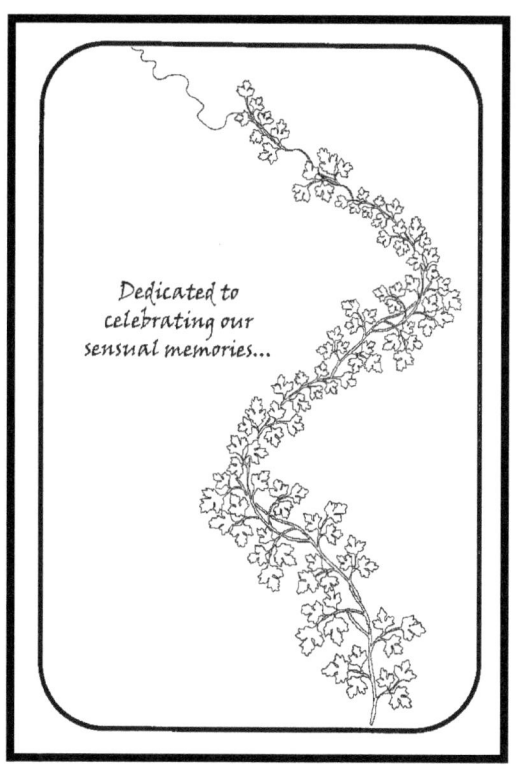

Dedicated to celebrating our sensual memories...

This book is dedicated to my lover, best friend and loving husband, Richard, whose sensual inspirations gave me wings to fly. To my kindred spirit, BJ, who gently nudged me to follow my dreams; Birt, my forever friend, who sparked my thunder and touched my spirit during those late night talks that meant so much. To my brothers, Dick and Norman, who always believed in my adventures and provided those constant rainbows residing in my head. To my lifelong friend, Pat, for sharing so much and walking by my side, and especially to my son, Brent, for his subtle, strong reserve and the eternal belief in his eyes.

Acknowledgements

My close friend, Dar, who passed away days before this book went to the publisher. She fanned the flame and allowed me to be myself. I thank her for all the years she pushed and encouraged me to write, to paint, and to motivate others. She will always reside in my heart.

To my sister-in-law, Pat, who did not get to see this book come alive. She was my creative genius who felt my words deeply and created the perfect journey to make it real with her graphics that suited my poetry.

Sisterhood

Intoxicating Rhapsody

I pay homage to the women who have supported me through my journey

Journey with me
Beckon to my fanciful
kaleidoscope
I am bedraggled, bursting and
succulent
Oh cylinder of my heartbeats
Moaned through the sultry sound
of the chanteuse
Deepened by your stillness

Heady Scent of Lilac

Nostalgic Progression

*A lady's hat speaks long
before she can utter a sound*

In my past life
I took many lovers

Laid back and drank
The grace notes of music made

Held spellbound in my passing fancy
Met by a touch of hand
Undone by passion's rage

Loved so many and loved them all
In this life so lives the memories

Ossie, I have loved her since I was a child

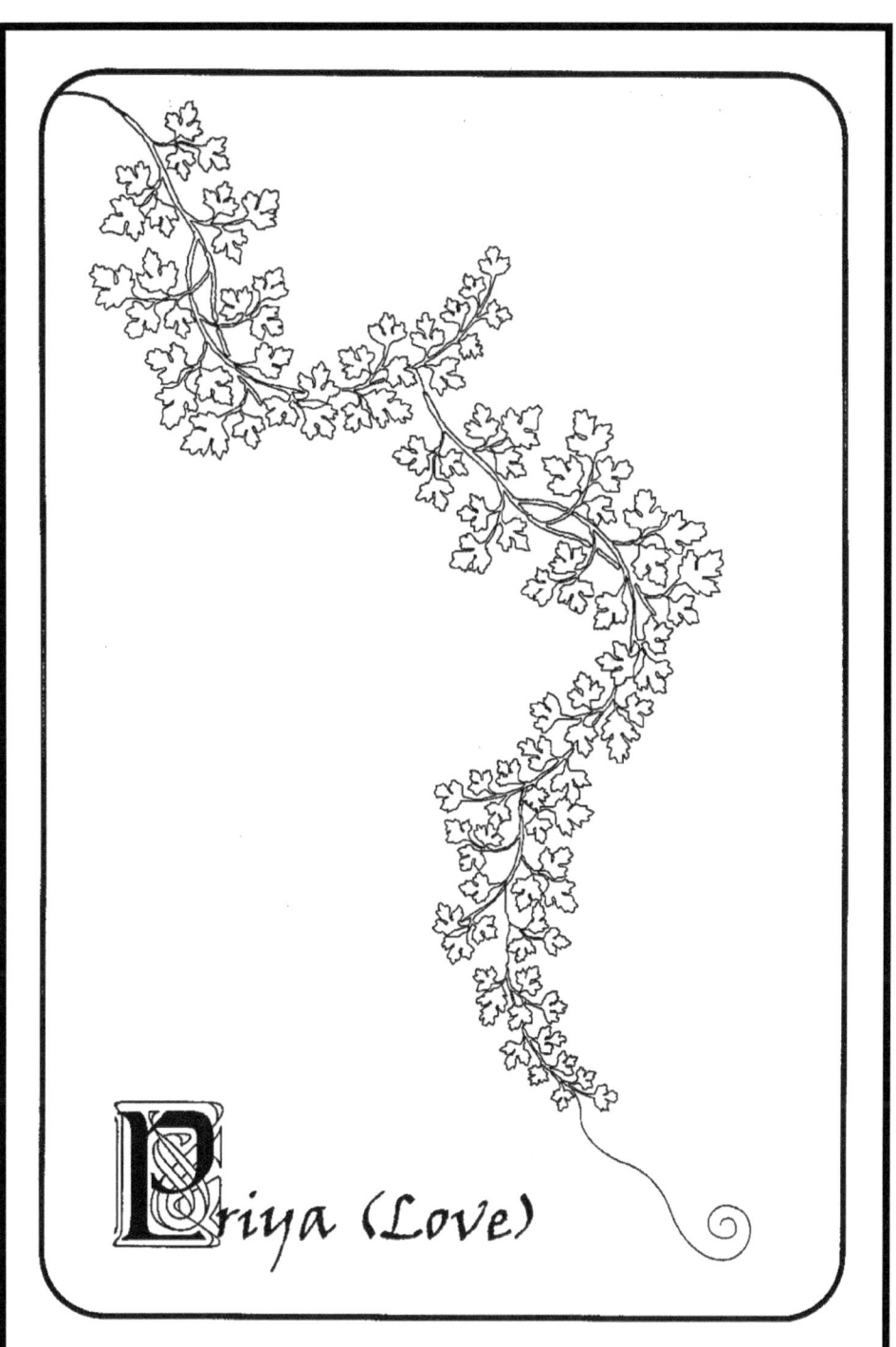

Priya (Love)

My lilac goddess who stands by my side always

Launched by spirits of centuries rest; Awaked in the depth of stillness; Quiet and calm stopped the passage; Inside a restless storm; Savor the forbidden moments; Held captive in a distant sound. Realization flooding heartbeats; Overwhelming enraptured longing; Sated with impetuous fullness; Unleash my desirous passion; My far away captive keeper.

Alone but not lonely

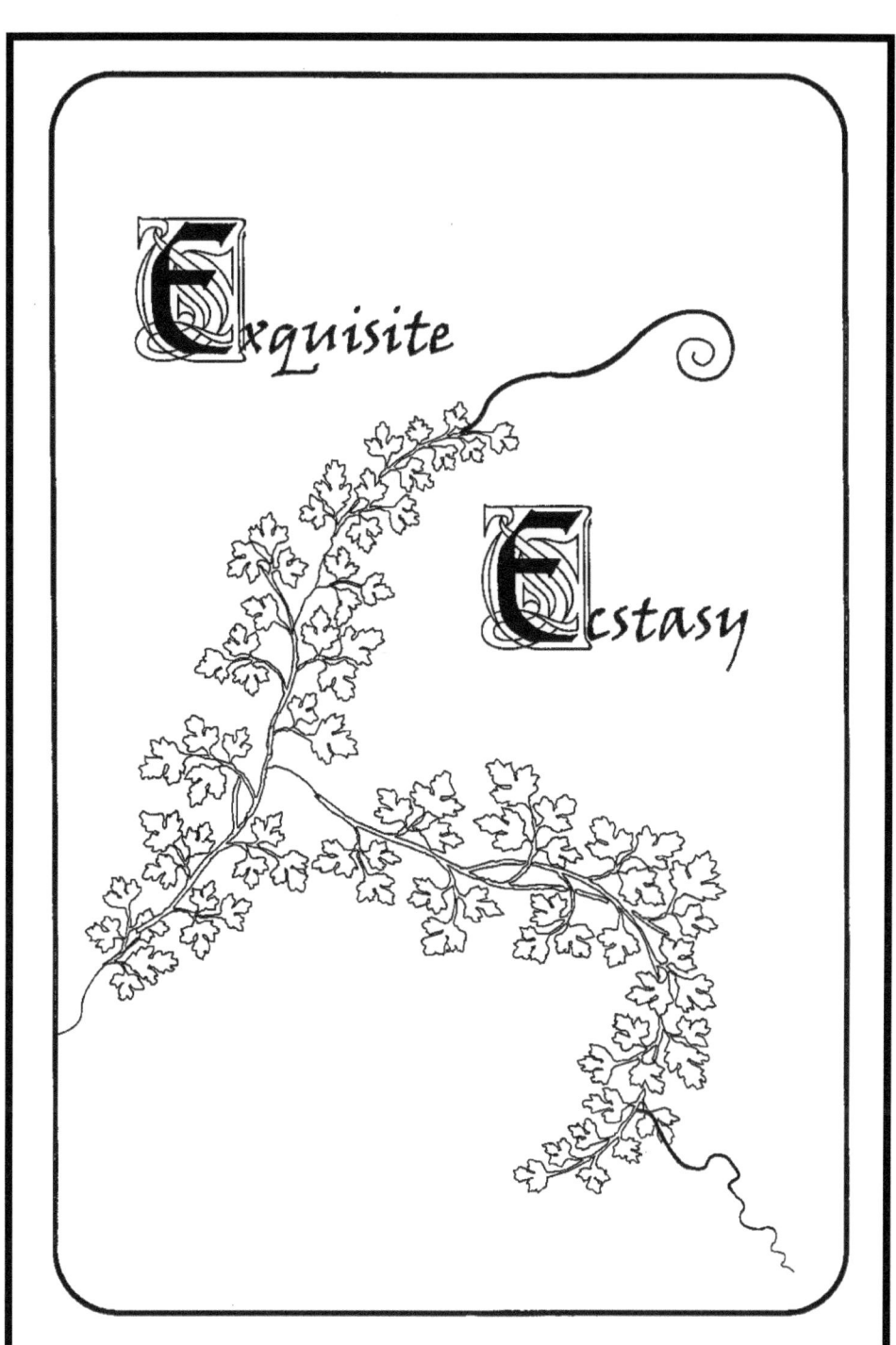

Exquisite Ecstasy

This adorned image inspired me to paint my feelings in quiet boldness

Resounding spent desires
Aroused another time
Remembered in the moment
Undo a secret place
Beckoned to my lover
Feelings of smothering drifts
Release my passive stirrings
Touch my molten moments
Electrify my senses

I lean on her in all that I do

*In the still of night when all is asleep
I paint the sounds of serenity*

Yesteryear a lover
Paused in restless pride
Undo my realm of senses
Admission to desires
Held captive by a fancy
Burst of plenitude

Far away lover
Heightened my desire
Tasted the joys of nectar
Relinquished by submission

Finding my moments of calmness

Trilogy of Love

These exuberant women are often seen in my paintings, they will not be ignored

Many revolutions
Still my heart
Aches with burning desire
You are every hour my new love

Dance away lover
Eyes meet
I see in you all my pleasures
Renewed by each breath

Trappings evolved with passing of time
Within my soul and spirit
I am motionless
Envy our first quiver
Arouse me still

Good friends who stand by me

Enraptured

The joy of reinventing myself

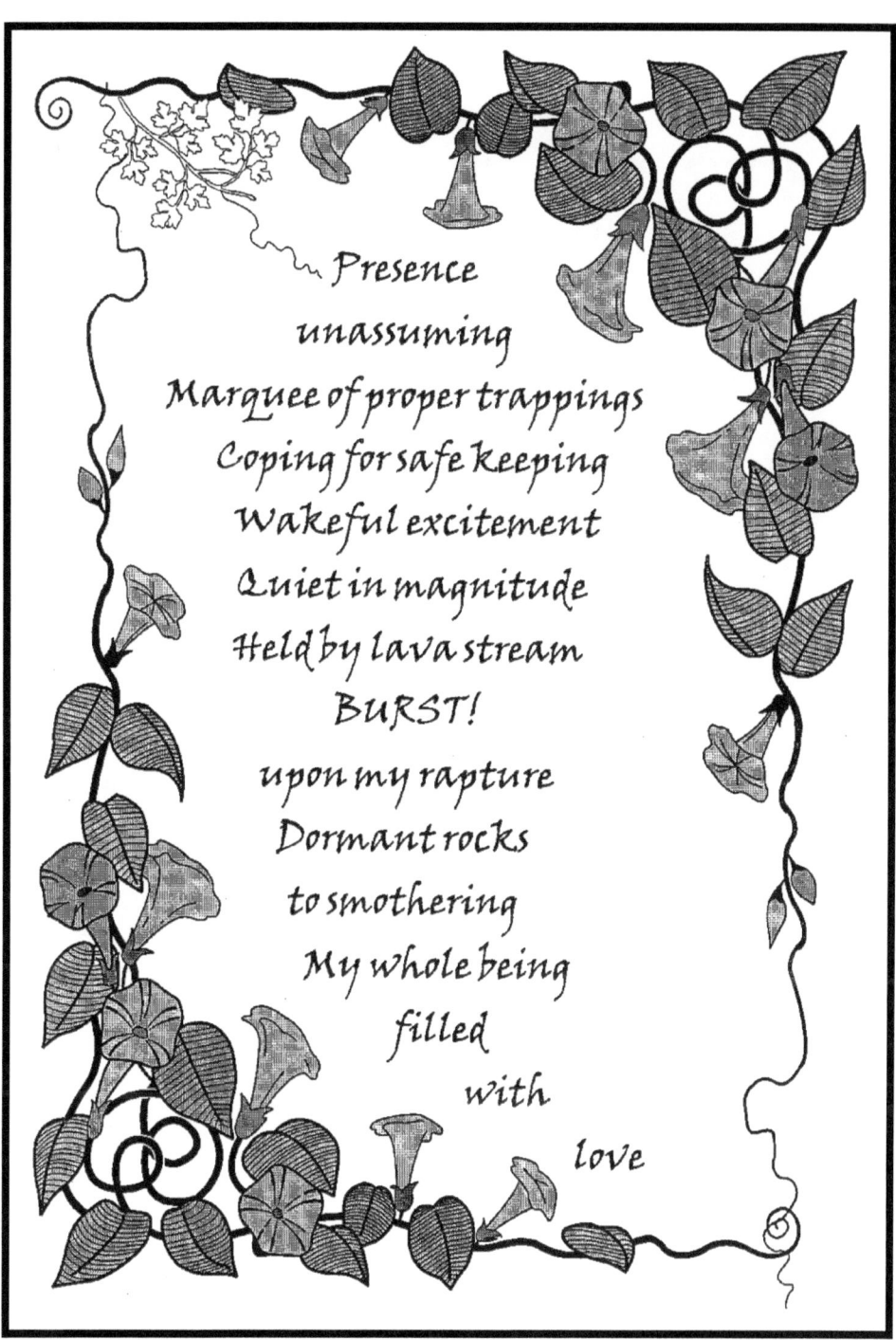

Presence
unassuming
Marquee of proper trappings
Coping for safe keeping
Wakeful excitement
Quiet in magnitude
Held by lava stream
BURST!
upon my rapture
Dormant rocks
to smothering
My whole being
filled
with
love

Within me is my mystery

Finding comfort in kinship

Called my strong love
Called my pure love
Called my only love
Called my eternal love
Called my best love
Called my undaunted love
Called my shameless love
Called my real love
Called my raw love
Called my forever love

I painted these women with these words in mind, soft, gentle and kind

Savory Glimpse

The presence of women dominates my work and ignites my imagination

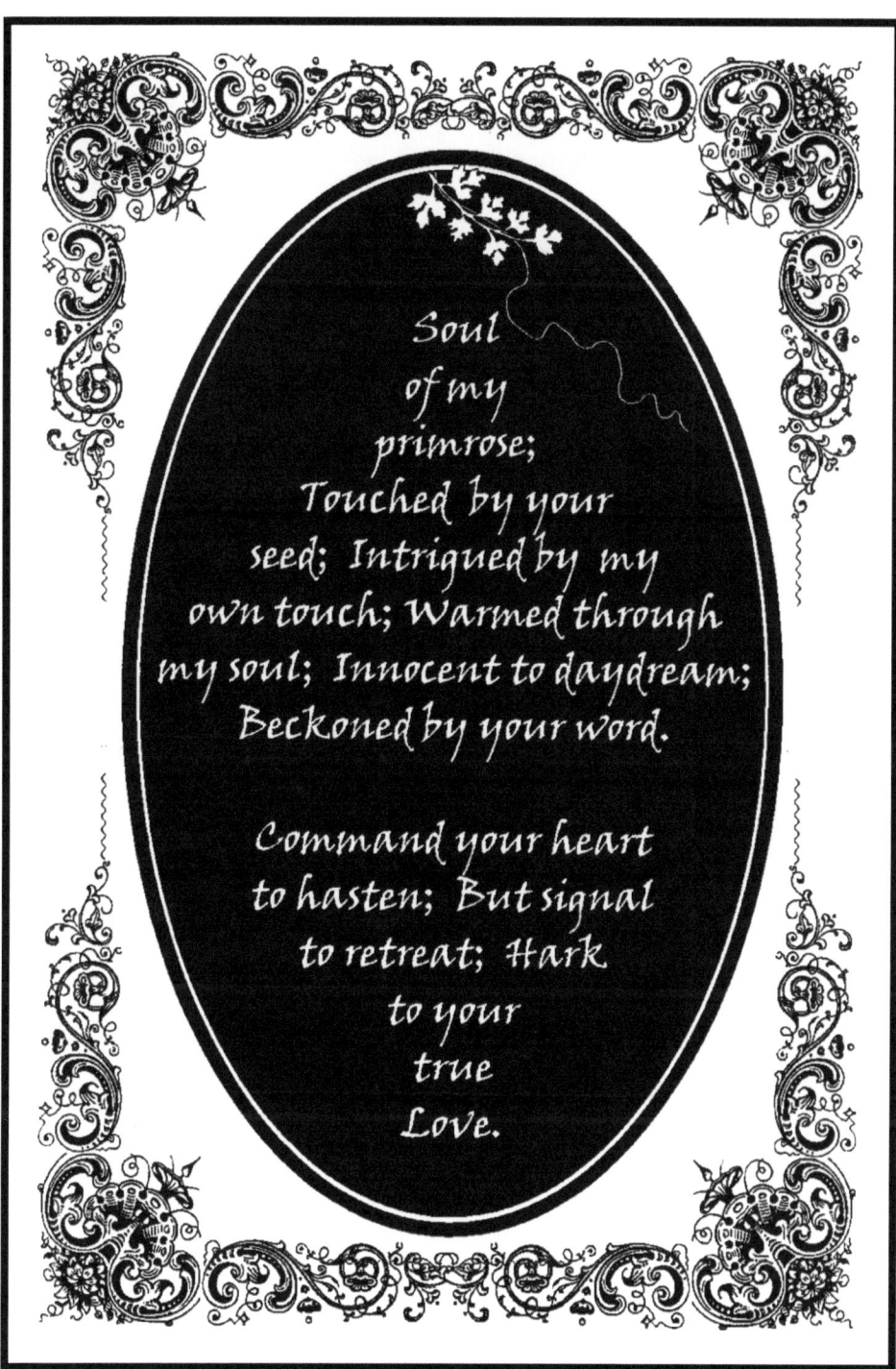

Soul
of my
primrose;
Touched by your
seed; Intrigued by my
own touch; Warmed through
my soul; Innocent to daydream;
Beckoned by your word.

Command your heart
to hasten; But signal
to retreat; Hark
to your
true
Love.

I aspired to capture an emotional likeness

Candid Splendor

*Bold colors assured me that together
we could do so much*

With each moment you bring renewal; Images of your influence; Catch a glimpse; Love below my surface; Passion abounds; Imbue with magic; Far away keeper

Women in church hats gave me my strength

Victorian Moments

Dedicated to all the mature women who sometimes feel invisible

Beloved past and present
Enslaving my uncertainty
Warm tears overflowing
Touched my heart
Strong to your eyes
Softened with grace

Speak to me of young love
But surrender to time
Oh! moments in the universe
Rarefied within
Struggle to understand our romance
Made one by Reflections

You know my face
Read my thoughts
Feel my joy
Reflect my sadness
Share my triumph

Feeling free to feel

Antiquity Ardor

My sister spirit

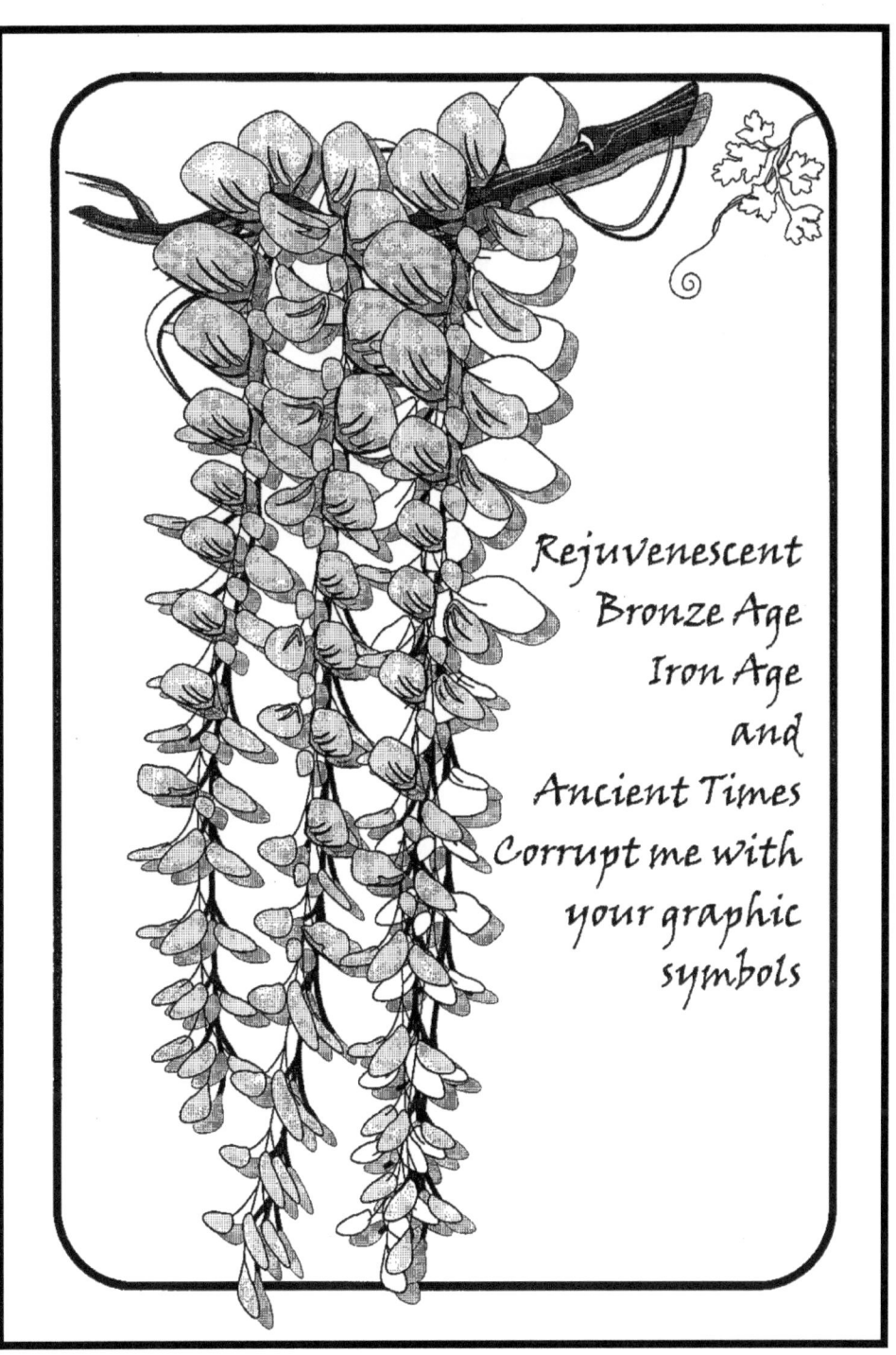

Rejuvenescent
Bronze Age
Iron Age
and
Ancient Times
Corrupt me with
your graphic
symbols

From generation to generation,
I celebrate you

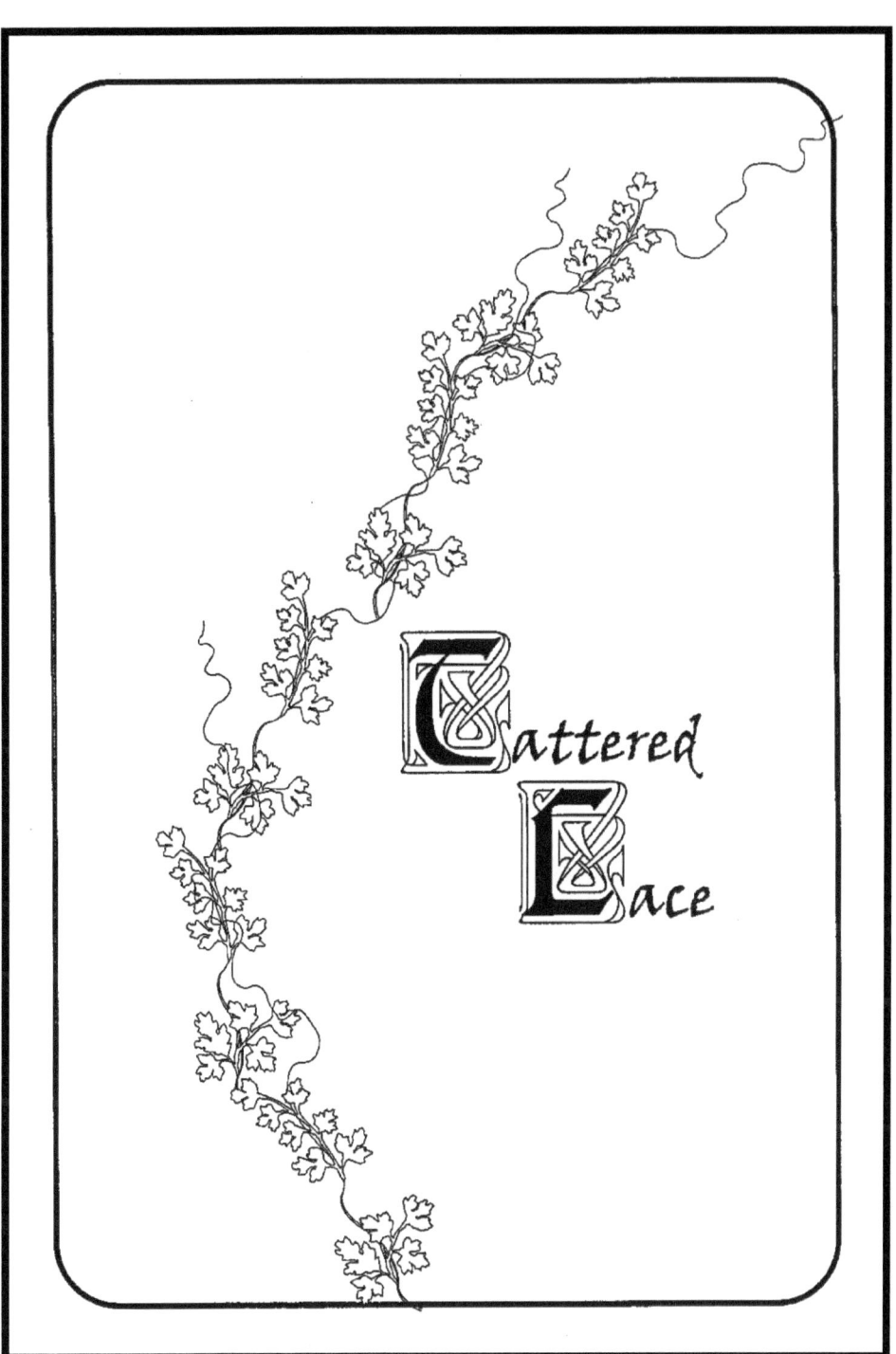

Tattered Lace

Kindred spirit

Exquisite enchantment
Verboten in name
Lurid sensations cloaked in delicacy
Undo my cloistered image
Murmur within my heartbeats
Moan by my side
Forbidden lover
Intoxicate my daydreams
For I am delirious with desire
Overcome by longing
Enraptured with wanting
Runneth over with fancy

I often find my courage when I hold myself close and listen

Delilah

This is where my many thoughts and feelings reside

Vintage lovers
Remembrances of flavors past
Magic potion
Bold, risky and discreet
Embodiment of who I am
Defined by how I feel
Stroke away my pretense
Languish between my
intoxicating aroma
Strip me of all proprieties
Tarnish who I am
Fill me with your memory
Call me Delilah

I cherish this childhood friend who gifted me with love and respect for the environment

About the Author

Dorothy Atkins

Years of commuting to work by train into San Francisco allowed many free hours to tap into my love of writing and drawing. There is only a fine line between what inspires me to put words to paper and paint on a canvas. My collection of poetry and artwork comes from stories and people who have left an impression on my life. This collection of art and poetry is a perfect journey that allowed the magic to ignite my dreams. Deep into my heart and soul I have felt romance and love so completely.

To my readers, sit back and recall your moments, whether it was your first love, a special lover, a continuous love or a love that has sustained the test of time. These are feelings that allow us to connect with others. As a consummate romantic I am a writer who also paints. My poetry is much like a painting on an intimate scale. My paintings are inspired by the rich diversity in this ride and the pure joy of experiencing different cultures.

www.ingramcontent.com/pod-product-compliance
Lightning Source LLC
Chambersburg PA
CBHW042310150426
43198CB00001B/30